Frank and Jesse James in the Civil War:
Who Became Outlaws of the Wild West

By Sean McLachlan & Charles River Editors

Jesse and Frank James

About the Author

Sean McLachlan has spent much of his life in Arizona and Missouri, working as an archaeologist and tracing legends of the Old West. Now a full-time writer, he's the author of many history books and novels, including *A Fine Likeness*, a Civil War novel with a touch of the weird and Jesse James as a character. Feel free to visit him on his Amazon page and blog.

About Charles River Editors

Charles River Editors provides superior editing and original writing services across the digital publishing industry, with the expertise to create digital content for publishers across a vast range of subject matter. In addition to providing original digital content for third party publishers, we also republish civilization's greatest literary works, bringing them to new generations of readers via ebooks.

Sign up here to receive updates about free books as we publish them, and visit Our Kindle Author Page to browse today's free promotions and our most recently published Kindle titles.

Introduction

Jesse James

"No more terrifying object ever came down a street than a mounted guerrilla wild for blood, the bridle-reins between his teeth or over the saddle-horn, the horse running recklessly, the rider yelling like a Comanche, his long unkempt hair flying wildly beyond the brim of his broad hat, and firing both to the right and left with deadly accuracy. When a town was filled with such men bent on death, terror ensued, reason and judgment fled, and hell yawned." - William Elsey Connelley, author of *Quantrill and the Border Wars*

The Civil War is best remembered for the big battles and the legendary generals who fought on both sides, like Robert E. Lee facing off against Ulysses S. Grant in 1864. In kind, the Eastern theater has always drawn more interest and attention than the West. However, while massive armies marched around the country fighting each other, there were other small guerrilla groups that engaged in irregular warfare on the margins.

Among these partisan bushwhackers, none are as infamous as William Quantrill and Quantrill's Raiders. Quantrill's Raiders operated along the border between Missouri and Kansas, which had been the scene of partisan fighting over a decade earlier during the debate over whether Kansas and Nebraska would enter the Union as free states or slave states. In "Bleeding Kansas", zealous pro-slavery and anti-slavery forces fought each other, most notably John

Brown, and the region became a breeding ground for Unionists and pro-slavery factions who shifted right back into similar fighting once the Civil War started. Rather than target military infrastructure or enemy soldiers, the bushwhackers rode in smaller numbers and targeted civilians on the other side of the conflict, making legends out of men like Bloody Bill Anderson and John Mosby.

Though Quantrill's Raiders were named after their famous leader William Clark Quantrill, the most notorious of the Raiders was none other than Jesse James. Frank and Jesse James have become American legends for their daring robberies and narrow escapes from the law, and many people, especially in the South, see them as folk heroes, unreconstructed rebels fighting for the Lost Cause against rich Northern bankers and capitalists. While that last bit is a matter for debate, the James brothers did indeed consider themselves Southern rebels at heart.

The Wild West has made legends out of many men after their deaths, but like Wild Bill Hickok, Jesse James was a celebrity during his life. However, while Hickok was (mostly) a lawman, Jesse James was and remains the most famous outlaw of the Wild West, with both his life of crime and his death remaining pop culture fixtures. James and his notorious older brother Frank were Confederate bushwhackers in the lawless region of Missouri during the Civil War. Despite being a teenager, Jesse James was severely wounded twice during the war, including being shot in the chest, but that would hardly slow him down after the war ended.

Eventually, Quantrill's Raiders headed south, and they eventually split off into several groups. Quantrill himself was killed while fighting in June 1865, nearly two months after Lee surrendered to Grant at Appomattox, but his name was kept alive by the notorious deeds of his Raiders during the war and the criminal exploits of former Raiders like Jesse and Frank James, as well as the Younger brothers. These men became some of America's most famous outlaws, and they used guerrilla tactics to rob banks and trains while eluding capture.

While their robberies were conducted more to enrich themselves than to strike back against the North, their rebel credentials were impeccable. The brothers came from a secessionist, slaveholding family and both fought for the Confederacy in the bitterest guerrilla war the nation has ever seen. To understand their outlaw careers, and their enduring legacy, one must understand how Frank and Jesse James fought during the Civil War.

Frank and Jesse James in the Civil War: The History of the Bushwhackers Who Became Outlaws of the Wild West chronicles the history and events that involved the James brothers during the Civil War, and how the Civil War affected their lives as outlaws. Along with pictures of important people, places, and events, you will learn about the James brothers in the Civil War like never before, in no time at all.

Frank and Jesse James in the Civil War: The History of the Bushwhackers Who Became Outlaws of the Wild West

About the Author

About Charles River Editors

Introduction

   Chapter 1: Raised on a Bloody Border

   Chapter 2: Frank Goes to War

   Chapter 3: The Lawrence Massacre

   Chapter 4: Jesse Joins the Fight

   Chapter 5: A Bloody Ride across Missouri

   Chapter 6: A Final Gamble

   Chapter 7: Outlaws

Online Resources

Bibliography

Chapter 1: Raised on a Bloody Border

In 1842, the Reverend Robert James, father of America's most famous outlaws, moved his family from Kentucky to a farm near Kearney, in Clay County, western Missouri. Robert worked hard and prospered, laboring in his fields alongside his few slaves as was common practice in Missouri at that time. The state boasted few of the large plantations common in places like Mississippi and Louisiana, and most slave owners only had one or two slaves. Slaves made up just under 10% of Missouri's population in 1860.

The James Farm in Kearney

On Sundays, Robert James preached at the local Baptist church, and his sermons grew popular thanks to his mixture of strong oratory and down-home wisdom. Like many churches, the Baptist creed was split on the issue of slavery, and Robert used his pulpit to fulminate against the abolitionists.

In 1843, his wife Zerelda gave birth to their first son, who they named Frank. Another son named Jesse arrived in 1847. Neither would grow up with their father, who left when they were still children, lured by the gold fields of California, where he soon died in poverty. Their mother was made of strong stuff and raised the boys and ran the farm more or less alone, remarrying twice to quiet men she easily dominated. The second husband was of little account and quickly forgotten by the close-knit family. The third, Dr. Rueben Samuel, a mild-mannered doctor who gave up his medical practice to grow hemp and tobacco at the James farm, stayed with Zerelda until his death and was loved by the boys, although he didn't make much of a father figure.

Zerelda James

The James brothers grew up in a region that was becoming deeply divided. In the 1850s, the social nature of Missouri changed rapidly due to an influx of immigrants. Many hailed from northern states and differed with southerners over the issue of slavery. Joining them were tens of thousands of foreigners, including a large number of Germans, who were fleeing totalitarian governments at home and saw slavery as just another form of oppression.

Missouri began to fill up, and the newcomers turned their eyes westwards towards the open prairie of Kansas. Southerners were concerned to see so many northerners moving into the Territory of Kansas and feared that when it became a state, it would become a Free State, banning slavery. This would mean Missouri would be surrounded on three sides by Free States, an implicit threat to the institution of slavery in Missouri and making it far too easy for their human chattel to escape.

Missourians began to take matters into their own hands, heading across the state line en masse to vote in territorial elections and intimidate Free State voters. In the November 1854 election, about half the votes cast were by these temporary Kansans. Another election in March 1855 saw 6,307 ballots cast when there were in fact only 2,905 registered voters. Only 791 voted to make slavery illegal in the territory. Those who did vote for a Free State ran the risk of having their farms burned, or worse.

In response, abolitionist organizations such as the New England Emigrant Aid Society began to fund northern immigrant wagon trains, providing them with Sharps rifles in case they got attacked. Unlike most rifles at the time, these could shoot several shots without reloading and were accurate to a long range. With them, the Free Staters threatened to take over the territory.

Tensions rose and the bloodshed increased. Proslavery Missourians called bushwhackers raided Kansas, killing Free State settlers and burning abolitionist newspaper offices. In turn, antislavery Kansas Jayhawkers raided western Missouri, killing slave owners and freeing their human property. Several Clay County farms suffered from Jayhawker raids, although the James farm itself was never attacked.

The Free State side gradually gained the upper hand. By the summer of 1855, the New England Emigrant Aid Society had sent some 1,200 northerners to Kansas, and many more were arriving through their own resources. They began to outnumber the proslavery residents, and while the fighting continued, the bushwhackers found their raids coming up against tough resistance.

In September of 1856, the new territorial governor, John Geary, arrived and began to push for the territory to be admitted into the Union as a Free State. He called in the military to help push the bushwhackers out. It wasn't until July of 1859, however, before the territory adopted a Free State constitution, and Kansas wasn't admitted as such until 1861, after the South had seceded.

Geary

The struggle, known as Bleeding Kansas, was a prequel to the American Civil War. All across the young nation, Americans took sides on the slavery issue, digging in their heels as moderate voices got drowned out. When Abraham Lincoln was elected president in 1860, newspapers and politicians across the South proclaimed that he would abolish slavery. It didn't matter that Lincoln said he only wanted to stop it from spreading to new territories, his election alone was proof in their minds that the North intended on crushing the South by taking their slaves, economically hamstringing it.

Then came the breaking point. South Carolina seceded from the Union on December 20, 1860, stating in its articles of secession that the Northern states had avoided their legal obligations by not returning escaped slaves and that, "they have denounced as sinful the institution of slavery; they have permitted open establishment among them of societies, whose avowed object is to disturb the peace and to eloign the property of the citizens of other States. They have encouraged and assisted thousands of our slaves to leave their homes; and those who remain, have been incited by emissaries, books and pictures to servile insurrection. For twenty-five years this agitation has been steadily increasing, until it has now secured to its aid the power of the common Government. . . A geographical line has been drawn across the Union, and all the States north of that line have united in the election of a man to the high office of President of the United States, whose opinions and purposes are hostile to slavery. He is to be entrusted with the administration of the common Government, because he has declared that that 'Government cannot endure permanently half slave, half free,' and that the public mind must rest in the belief that slavery is in the course of ultimate extinction."

Mississippi came next on January 9, 1861, stating in its own declaration of secession, "In the momentous step which our State has taken of dissolving its connection with the government of which we so long formed a part, it is but just that we should declare the prominent reasons which have induced our course. Our position is thoroughly identified with the institution of slavery--the greatest material interest of the world. Its labor supplies the product which constitutes by far the largest and most important portions of commerce of the earth." Florida, Alabama, Georgia, Louisiana, Texas, Virginia, Arkansas, North Carolina and Tennessee followed. Their articles of secession were similarly worded. They would rather create their own nation than risk giving up the right of the individual states to decide on the slavery issue.

The United States had broken apart.

Chapter 2: Frank Goes to War

Having already learned an early lesson in internecine strife, Missourians were prepared for war, and yet they were split on the idea of secession. Their state was a mixed one, with the majority of rural people favoring secession while the majority of residents in the urban areas of St. Louis, Columbia, and Kansas City favored staying in the Union. There wasn't a county or town, however, which was all one or the other. It was truly a state divided.

The Missouri state government, led by Governor Claiborne Fox Jackson, was strongly secessionist but worried about Missouri's geographic position, exposed as it was on three sides by the Unionist states of Illinois, Iowa, and Kansas. They bided their time, saying that Missouri would be neutral but would defend itself if the federal government invaded. Secretly, however, Jackson contacted the new Confederate government at Richmond, Virginia, asking for weapons. He and his lieutenant governor, Thomas Reynolds, planned to seize the large federal arsenal in St. Louis. As Jackson called up the Missouri State Guard, Congressman Frank Blair organized a Unionist Home Guard militia in St. Louis made of up loyalist German immigrants. Across the state, men of both sides began to organize their own volunteer companies.

Jackson

On March 4, 1861, the day Lincoln was inaugurated in Washington, Missouri held a state convention on the issue of secession. Debate raged until March 22, when the convention returned a vote of 98-1 against leaving the United States. But that didn't end the issue. Congressman Blair narrowly avoided assassination, and when news came of the bombardment of Fort Sumter and Lincoln's call for 75,000 troops to suppress the rebellion, many Missourians who sat on the fence swung in favor of the South. While they didn't fully approve of secession, they would not condone the use of force to stop it and felt the federal government had gone too far.

Clay County was a hotbed of secessionism. Its people mostly hailed from slave states and had been embittered by the raids of Bleeding Kansas. A mob captured the federal arsenal at the county seat of Liberty on April 20, while speakers across the county held meetings calling for Missouri's break from the Union. The Southern cause was given a further shot in the arm on May 10. The Missouri State Guard, numbering 890 men, had camped near the federal arsenal in St. Louis. The commander of Blair's new Home Guard forces, Brigadier-General Nathaniel Lyon, a strong Unionist who had helped pacify Kansas, correctly suspected the State Guard had their eyes set on the federal arsenal. When he captured a secret shipment of siege mortars sent by the Confederate States of America, he decided to act.

Lyon

On May 10, Lyon led his 3,000 men, including regular troops and German-American Home Guards, to the parade ground where the militia was camped and quickly surrounded them. Outnumbered and poorly armed, the militia had no choice but to surrender. As the victorious troops marched their prisoners back into the city, an angry mob gathered around and started insulting Lyon's men. Catcalls and spit escalated into a hail of rocks. Then someone fired a shot at the Unionist troops. The troops fired back, and when the smoke cleared, 28 civilians lay dead. The next day there was more rioting, with a further seven civilians killed.

The St. Louis Massacre, as the secessionists called it, galvanized secessionists across the state, and Frank James was caught up in the excitement. In early May, secessionists in Clay County formed a local militia and he was one of its first recruits. Jesse, being only 13, wasn't able to enlist.

The Clay County militia joined the Missouri State Guard that same month, marching down to the southwestern part of the state to drill along with thousands of other wide-eyed men, both young and old. There was no longer any pretense at moderation. The Missouri State Guard, led by former governor and Mexican War veteran Major-General Sterling Price, would fight for the Confederacy, even if Missouri was still technically in the Union.

Price

While many of the men would have been farmers and familiar with guns, this was an amateur army. There were almost no experienced officers, and the quartermaster department struggled to feed the new recruits and could distribute few weapons and no uniforms. The new soldiers drilled in the clothes they had left home with, shouldering sticks with knives lashed to the ends if they hadn't had the foresight to bring an old shotgun or rifle with them.

They weren't lacking in enthusiasm, however. In those early months, almost everyone on both sides thought the war would be quick and glorious. They wanted a fight and they were soon to get it. Lyon acted quickly, moving west out of St. Louis along the Missouri River in a flotilla of steamboats. He took the state capital, Jefferson City, without a shot on June 15 and defeated a small State Guard force at the prosperous river port of Boonville on June 17. Jackson and his secessionist government fled, heading down to the southwestern corner of the state to the safety of Price's gathering army.

Skirmishes sparked all across Missouri as rival militias attacked each other, but the first sizeable battle occurred near the town of Carthage on July 5. An overconfident Union force of 1,100 men tried to stand against the main force of the Missouri State Guard, which fielded 6,000 men, of whom only 4,000 were armed. After a long day's fighting, the Union army was forced to retreat. While it was no major victory, it temporarily weakened the Union presence in southwestern Missouri, buoyed up the Missouri State Guards' spirits, increased recruitment, and made Sterling Price a Southern hero. It's unclear if Frank was at this battle. He never seems to have mentioned it, but he was part of the Missouri State Guard by this time. Perhaps he had other duties that day, or perhaps the larger battles to come made him overlook this fight when talking about his war years.

A bloodier battle followed soon after. Early on the morning of August 10, Price's army was camped at Wilson's Creek, 12 miles southwest of General Lyon's base at Springfield. The Missouri State Guard now numbered some 12,000 men, including Frank James, and camping with them were troops from Arkansas, Texas, and Louisiana. The morning dawned peaceful and quiet. The army was just waking up. Men made breakfast or went down to the creek to wash or fetch water for coffee. Just then there was a roar of musket and cannon fire. Panicked men fled from the outer edges of the camp inwards, desperately seeking safety.

Lyon's force had appeared, some 5,400 men who had made a rapid march out of Springfield to catch Price by surprise. The Union troops were better armed, but they were a mix of U.S. regular troops and new volunteers from Missouri, Kansas, and Iowa.

Despite having the smaller force, Lyon divided his army, simultaneously attacking Price's camp from the north and south. From the south came a small force led by Colonel Franz Sigel. An experienced artillery officer, this German-American was soon laying down an accurate fire into the disorganized rebels. From the north came the bulk of the Union army, led by General Lyon himself. Lyon's men quickly took a hill overlooking Price's camp, set up their artillery, and started sending shells down into the tents.

Sigel

For the young Frank James, it must have been a frightening experience. The Yankees were attacking from two sides, and no one yet realized the disparity in numbers. Luckily Price kept his head and ordered an advance in both directions. Frank's unit was one of many sent up the steep, brushy slopes of the hill to take it back from Lyon's men. As the men struggled up the hill, they faced fierce resistance from the Union troops. Frank's new friends began to fall all around him. The rebels formed a line and sent several volleys into the enemy before advancing, only to hurry back downhill in the face of a determined counterattack. Frank and his comrades regrouped and pushed back up. The fight would move back and forth like this for several hours, with heavy losses on both sides. Soon that hill would be known to everyone in Missouri as "Bloody Hill."

While Lyon was holding his own, things weren't going too well for Sigel. Through the haze of his cannons he saw a regiment advancing wearing gray uniforms. At this point in the war, uniforms hadn't been standardized, so men marched to battle wearing a wide variety of uniforms. Many Union men wore gray, and Sigel, knowing that the majority of rebels wore no uniforms at all, assumed these gray-clad troops were reinforcements sent to help him. In fact they were the 3rd Louisiana, who got to almost pointblank range before revealing their political beliefs with a devastating volley that tore through Sigel's ranks. His men buckled and ran for their lives, and Sigel mounted a horse and galloped all the way back to Springfield.

Now Price could focus all his troops on Bloody Hill. As the fighting grew ever fiercer, with both generals urging their men on from the front lines, Lyon was struck down by a bullet. He had already shrugged off two minor wounds, but this third gunshot was fatal. Command fell to Major Samuel Sturgis. Seeing his men had run low on ammunition and no longer hearing any fighting coming from Sigel's portion of the battlefield, he did the only thing he could do: order a retreat.

Sturgis

Frank must have breathed a sigh of relief. He had fought all day on Bloody Hill, firing and ducking during that seesaw slugfest under the punishing Missouri summer sun. In a newspaper interview much later in life, he scoffed that it was "a mighty slow fight". It was anything but. The rebels lost some 1,200 men that day, the Union about 1,300. Both armies were literally decimated, and most of the dead and wounded lay on that hillside. If Frank hadn't had his baptism of fire at Carthage, he certainly got it at Wilson's Creek.

The Union army returned to Springfield. Price, seeing the exhausted state of his own army, decided not to pursue. He had been handed a victory and did not want to risk turning it into a defeat. However, when he saw the Union army retreating further, Price decided to press his advantage and marched back to central Missouri. His goal was the Missouri River.

Price's army marched with little resistance to the river port of Lexington. He arrived on September 12 to find a Union force numbering 3,500 under Colonel James Mulligan dug in on a hill overlooking town. Strengthening their position at the top of the hill was the stone building of the local Masonic College. Mulligan, although greatly outnumbered, decided to hold on and wait for reinforcements. Price attacked immediately but was repulsed by accurate fire from the earthworks. Seeing that his tired men, low on ammunition, needed rest and refitting, he surrounded the hill and started foraging in the countryside.

Mulligan

The news that Price's army had captured an important port on the Missouri River electrified the state. New recruits poured in from surrounding farms. As Price's artillery bombarded the hilltop, his men encircled Mulligan's position and sniped at the defenders. They didn't dare a frontal assault up the open slope against the entrenched Union troops, so for a time there were few casualties on either side. The Union defenders kept the attackers at a distance with well-placed rifle shots, and their artillery fired on the rebel positions. One cannonball went long and embedded itself in a column of the local courthouse, where it can be seen to this day.

For several days it was a standoff as both sides waited to see who would be reinforced first. Frank James must have found this siege a bit dull after the hard fighting at Wilson's Creek. He did his share on the firing line, though, keeping up the pressure on the Union defenders in the hope that they would surrender.

In the end, they would not. Many were experienced soldiers, and Mulligan was a career officer with a firm loyalty to his country. He had no intention of giving up, and he spent many an anxious hour scanning the horizon for the relief force he felt was sure to come. In fact, three small forces had been sent by the high command in St. Louis, but they were beaten back or turned away without a fight at the sight of Price's swelling army.

On September 18, the waiting game ended when a wagon train of ammunition and other supplies for the Missouri State Guard made it Price's camp. Now he was ready to strike. He ordered an assault that took a strategic house at the base of the hill and also a nearby spring that was the garrison's only water supply. Now Mulligan and his men were in desperate straits. They tried to dig wells within their lines but didn't strike water. The only water they had left was whatever was in the barrels and buckets, and that was diminishing quickly.

Price, however, could not wait for the defenders to succumb to thirst. He feared a stronger relief force might come, and so on September 20 ordered a full-scale assault. The attack was assisted by a novel new tactic. Lexington was at the heart of Missouri's hemp growing industry. Before hemp was banned in the 20th century because of its alternative use as marijuana, it was a major cash crop in the United States, with Missouri as one of the main suppliers. Hemp was used for everything from clothing and sails to paper and rope. The hemp harvest had just come in, and Lexington's docks groaned under the weight of countless bales of the fibrous plant.

Someone hit on the idea of using the bales as a mobile barrier, and soon a wall of hemp bales was moving up the hill. Men crouched behind it, rolling the heavy bales up the slope. Bullets couldn't pass through them, while a lucky shot with a cannonball only made a bale rock back a bit. Soon it was all over. As the moving wall approached the Union entrenchments, rebels fired from behind their protection. The defenders began to fall. Outnumbered, thirsty, cut off from the outside world, and on the verge of being overrun, they had no choice but to surrender.

The fall of Lexington was crucial to the Southern cause; not only was it an important river port, its capture opened up the road to the state capital and cut the vital lifeline of the Missouri River between St. Louis and Kansas City. While Price suspected the time was not yet ripe to take St. Louis, holding Lexington would isolate Kansas and give the secessionists the chance to take it, or at least neutralize the threat to their western border.

However, his optimism was soon dashed. Word came that a Union army numbering 38,000 had marched out of St. Louis, heading his way. Other detachments started to converge from the west and north. As Union forces closed in, Price saw his position was untenable, so on September 29, he reluctantly ordered a withdrawal back to southwestern Missouri. The siege of Lexington would prove to be the high water mark of the Confederacy in the state. Never again would a rebel army capture so much Missouri territory.

As the victorious but dispirited rebels trudged south, Frank fell ill with measles and was left in the care of a local family, but the pursuing Union troops soon caught up with him and took him prisoner. Frank and other captured stragglers were paroled, meaning they were allowed to return home in exchange for swearing not to fight. He and hundreds of others from Price's army ended up back at their farms. It seemed the war was over for them.

With the secessionist forces marginalized in the southern fringes of the state, and with their government hiding out with them, the old state convention reconvened on July 1861 and appealed to Lincoln to recognize it as the legitimate state government, a request the president was happy to approve. Now Missouri had two state governments. Small battles still occurred in various parts of the state, but the majority of the paroled Missouri State Guardsmen, Frank included, were stranded in a state that seemed all but controlled by the Union.

Nevertheless, a new type of war had begun. In the summer of 1861, secessionist guerrilla bands sprang up everywhere. They sniped at Union troops and trains, burned railway bridges, and cut telegraph wires. Neighbor turned on neighbor, and in many of the more secessionist communities, Unionists were driven out en masse. General Ulysses S. Grant was in Missouri that summer and recalled how Jefferson City was "filled with Union fugitives who had been driven by guerrilla bands to take refuge with the National troops. They were in a deplorable condition…They had generally made their escape with a team or two, sometimes a yoke of oxen with a mule or a horse in the lead. A little baggage besides their clothing and some food had been thrown into the wagon. All else of their worldly goods were abandoned and appropriated by their former neighbors."

Most of these guerrillas showed little inclination to join General Price's army. It was difficult to make it that far south without getting captured, and guerrilla warfare had its own appeal. The men could stay close to home, sometimes even working their fields by day and raiding by night, and they enjoyed the freedom of fighting in their own way without being burdened by military discipline. For some, the chance of grabbing some loot from their Unionist neighbors also proved tempting.

At the same time, secessionists were not the only ones acting this way. There were some Unionist guerrillas in Missouri, and many more coming from Kansas, including experienced fighters from the old Jayhawking days of Bleeding Kansas. They retained the name, and made it synonymous with outlawry even among most Unionists. As one Union officer wrote on December 31, 1861, he noted the town of Westport near Kansas City, which was the base for the notorious Jayhawking outfit under "Doc" Jennison, "was once a thriving town, with large stores, elegant private dwellings, and a fine large hotel. Now soldiers are quartered in the dwellings and horses occupy the storerooms. The hotel was burned down three days ago. The houses are torn to pieces…the mantles used to build fires, and doors unhinged. I presume the place will be burned as soon as the troops leave." The effect on the rural areas was even worse. As the officer noted, the areas where the Jayhawkers raided were left with "crops ungathered, houses deserted, barns and stables falling to pieces, fences torn down, and stock running loose and uncared for."

Jennison

Down in the southwestern town of Neosho, Governor Jackson and the remnants of the state government voted to join the Confederacy on October 30. The Confederate government officially approved the action on 28 November 1861. However, it was cold comfort for the organized forces of rebellion. In February 1862, Price's army fled the state at the approach of a larger Union army. The two forces finally clashed on March 7 and 8 at Pea Ridge, Arkansas, with the rebels getting badly mauled. The following month, the Missouri State Guard was disbanded, and Price and many of his men moved east of the river to fight for the Southern cause in other states.

At this stage, many of the paroled rebels lost hope. There seemed little chance that Price would return, and whatever occurred in the rest of the country, Missouri would be controlled by the Union. Frank and other former State Guardsmen must have felt the rest of the war would pass them by. Indeed, that might have been the case if the Unionist Missouri state government hadn't forced their hand. The countryside had come alive with Confederate guerrilla bands, who generally took the old Bleeding Kansas name of "bushwhackers". Some were officially recognized by the Confederate government, while many more were simply groups of adventurous young men who decided to fight the war "on their own hook". With Washington draining the state of Union troops to fight the big campaigns in the East, the local Unionist government badly needed men to keep order in the countryside. Thus, in July of 1862, it enacted General Order No. 19, commanding all able-bodied men to join their local Union militias. Called the Enrolled Missouri Militia, it would be a part-time service that freed the regular troops from more day-to-day affairs such as local garrison duty, guarding important local spots like bridges, and the increasingly dangerous job of escorting the mail.

The creation of the Enrolled Missouri Militia brought some 52,000 soldiers into the Union fold, including four companies in Clay County. Being a conscript force, the EMM was of varying quality. Some units were of dubious loyalty, and a few even mutinied. Others proved their mettle and faithfully fought for the Union. The only way out of joining the militia was to take a loyalty oath and pay a commutation tax of $10, which is what Frank and Jesse's stepfather, Reuben Samuel, decided to do. There was no way his strong-willed secessionist wife Zerelda would tolerate him joining a Yankee militia. But this, of course, made him instantly suspect in the eyes of the Unionist government. Frank had to go and register himself as disloyal, even though he had taken an oath of loyalty as a condition of his parole. While he avoided service in the militia, he was a marked man.

It was all too much for Frank. He, like countless others, decided to rejoin the fight on the side of the South. While some made their way across the lines to join Price or one of the other rebel commanders, Frank saw the life of a guerrilla as far more attractive. Not only would he be free of army discipline, but he could stay in Missouri.

In early May of 1863, Frank joined a small local guerrilla band. He wanted to see action, and he got it soon enough. On May 19, two drunken bushwhackers visited a house near Missouri City in Clay County. As they lounged around, they bragged to the owner about how they were members of Quantrill's guerrillas. The homeowner was a Union man, and he hurried into Missouri City to speak to Lieutenant Louis Gravenstein of the 25th Missouri Infantry, who had 16 men in town and was consulting with Captain Darius Sessions, head of the local Enrolled Missouri Militia. The pair was planning a sweep through the area to hunt for bushwhackers and when they heard about the man's unwelcome guests, they saw this as an easy opportunity to get valuable intelligence. In their eagerness to make the capture, they rushed out with only three soldiers.

It was all a trick, one of many the guerrillas would play on the overconfident Union troops throughout the war. As the five soldiers hurried down the road, a volley erupted out of the dense underbrush. Sessions and one of the other soldiers fell. The others tried to surrender and were killed. It was rare for the bushwhackers to take prisoners. As the war grew ever more bitter, it would become almost unheard of.

Once their quarry had been dispatched, the bushwhackers rode into Missouri City, drove out the remaining troops, and robbed the homes of local Unionists. For the next few days they ran roughshod over the region, often spending the night at Unionist farms holding the family prisoner before moving out the next day. On May 25 they camped near the James farm, where Frank's mother Zerelda served them hot meals and 15 year old Jesse begged to be allowed to join. They refused, saying he was too young, but consoled him by letting him reload their revolvers.

The local Union militia soon caught wind of where the bushwhackers were hiding out. It's unclear how they learned, considering that most of the county was for the South, but someone must have talked. Frank James had already been spotted riding with the bushwhackers, and if the group had been seen in the area of the James farm, perhaps the militia came to the obvious conclusion.

Either way, a force of militiamen showed up at the James farm. It was, as luck would have it, the same militia Rueben and Frank had avoided joining. The militia demanded to know where the bushwhackers were hiding. No one talked, so they beat the teenaged Jesse. When the boy still didn't tell them what they wanted, the soldiers turned on mild-mannered Reuben Samuel. They tied a rope around his neck, gave him a final chance to talk, and then slung the rope over the branch of a tree. Yanking on the rope, they lifted him into the air, let him dangle for a minute, and then dropped him to the ground. Then they repeated the torture.

Frank and Jesse's uncle, the Baptist minister William James, showed up out of concern when he heard both the bushwhackers and the militia were converging at the James farm. He wrote how he arrived to find Zerelda "making such an outcry and giving them such a tongue-lashing as only she could give." Fearful of what the militia might do to her, he tried to quiet her down, but Zerelda rounded on him and snapped, "How can I be still when they are hanging my husband?"

Eventually, Reuben Samuel broke. Lieutenant James Rogers, who was in the hanging crew, reported that "his memory brightened up, and he concluded to reveal the hiding place of the rebels. He led the boys into the woods a short distance, and there, squatted on the ground in a dense thicket, was discovered the whole band." There was a firefight, with five guerrillas killed and several more wounded before the remainder slipped away into the thick underbrush, leading the militia on a chase for several miles before they finally got away.

Both Rueben and Zerelda were arrested and hauled away. After spending a week in custody,

Zerelda signed a loyalty oath she had no intention of honoring and was allowed to return home. Rueben was let out on parole two weeks later, but he never recovered from his torture. Afterwards his friends and family said he was a changed man, apparently having suffered brain damage from his near-lynching and remaining somewhat addle-brained for the rest of his days.

Naturally, Jesse now wanted to join the guerrillas even more. He burned with a deep hatred for the North, but he was not yet ready to fight. Some accounts say the inexperienced boy even shot off the tip of a finger off while reloading a pistol that year, shouting out "Dingus!" in surprise and pain. Jesse James apparently never resorted to swearing, even when mutilating himself in an embarrassing manner. His brother and the other guerrillas never forgot the incident and called him Dingus for the rest of his life.

Chapter 3: The Lawrence Massacre

Jesse might not have been ready, but Frank was spoiling for revenge. He had survived the fight at the farm, even though he had lost his horse in the pell-mell flight to safety. His little group fled to the Sni-A-Bar wilderness on the border of Jackson and Lafayette counties, an almost impenetrable jumble of densely wooded hills and gullies, and there he came to the largest encampment of bushwhackers he had ever seen, commanded by the biggest name among that rough community: William Clarke Quantrill.

Quantrill

In the first months of the war, Quantrill, along with bushwhackers and Cherokees, acted as a reserve cavalry that hung back while the regular Confederate army fought the major battles. While Quantrill was technically a Confederate soldier at this point, and he fought bravely when called on to confront Union soldiers, he preferred to stay on the margins of the battle in order to plunder the battlefield. Quick riches still suited his taste, while marching to battle did not and never could.

In time, Walker's self-defense militia became Quantrill's own, and in "Quantrill Country," the western Missourian terrain characterized by flat open land dotted with woods that irregulars could dash into, the population of Missouri took care of Quantrill and other bushwhackers. Citizens fed, housed, and supplied the guerrillas, and when Union troops failed to penetrate the wilderness havens of the bushwhackers, Quantrill and the other bushwhackers emerged and sought shelter with the populace. The visits were frequent and took, on the surface, the appearance of many liberties with the citizenry's property. On closer inspection, however, citizens appeared to recount the episodes with pride and nostalgia. One citizen recalled the stories their grandfather told about the war: "[H]e would wake up in the night and see somebody in front of the fireplace taking off his boots. The, walking in his sock feet, the person would go into a room that was seldom used and go to bed. Sometime the outside door would be silently opened and clothes put inside the house. This was a sign they needed to be mended; and this my grandmother would do, and in a few days someone would call for them. Sometimes, when my grandfather went to the stable in the morning, he would find one of his horses gone and a strange one in its stall, usually lame, or one that had lost a shoe. As soon as the lameness was gone, my grandfather would replace the shoe. In a few days he would go again to the stable and there would be his own horse, and the other would be gone. This is the way our people helped each other."

Another important step taken by the Confederates in 1861 was the Partisan Ranger Act of 1861, which made no distinction between "partisans" and "guerrillas". In short, both groups were to report to Confederate armies and be integrated into their commands for operations, but the irregulars were expected to live behind enemy lines and switch between civilian clothes and military uniforms. Quantrill himself would hold a commission within the Confederate army but act independently. While the Partisan Ranger Act of 1861 means the establishment of these bushwhacker units can at least be partly blamed on the Confederate government, they were powerless to control Quantrill's Raiders. One of Quantrill's chief lieutenants, "Bloody Bill" Anderson, later said "I don't care any more than you for the South...but there is lot of money in this [bushwhacking] business."

Quantrill's Raiders could be categorically defined as men fighting for the Confederacy, states' rights, and slavery, but in most cases, the men actually saw the war as an opportunity to reinvent and enrich themselves. By the end of the war, the last of their numbers were mostly rogues who had found another way to occupy their libertine times. Vengeance against the Northern invaders unified them, and they chose violence as their medium of expression. Soldiering did not satiate the desire for bloodshed, but raiding and ambushing did.

One of Quantrill's most important associates was "Bloody Bill" Anderson, who made a knot in a silken rope for every man he killed. By the time he was killed in battle in late 1864, his rope had 54 knots. Anderson came from a family infamous for their predations on the Kansas prairies, specifically the Santa Fe Trail, and his father was shot dead by a judge over a stolen horse. With the law ready to throw Bill in jail, the family left for Missouri, where the hard life as a pirate of the plains made Anderson a tough man who colleagues said loved to kill. According to contemporaries, the act of violence provoked him to froth at the mouth, and he never spared a man's life.

Bloody Bill Anderson

Along with Anderson, handsome features also described George Todd, a Canadian whose love of killing was his most known characteristic. While Anderson was known for his long ringlets of black hair, Todd's blue eyes and blond hair made him stand out. Like Anderson, good looks contradicted his sinister deposition. Unlike Anderson's bloodthirsty familial ties, nothing seemed to suggest why Todd chose the life of a bushwhacker, but a partial explanation seemed to come in his young age during the move to Missouri. By the age of 18, his experiences on the frontier had led him to a life of theft and murder. Quantrill would rely on him more than other guerrilla, and eventually, he would rival Quantrill for leadership.

Thomas Coleman Younger, known as Cole Younger, came from a Missourian family like Jesse and Frank James. However, unlike the James brothers, Younger lived an easy life as the son of successful plantation and farm owner. His father never preached secession, but the depredations of Jayhawkers and their destruction of farm properties helped make up the patriarch's mind to support for the Confederacy. The family ran afoul of Union army occupiers who targeted Cole for his suspected rebel support, and a later Union raid against the Younger estates left Cole's father dead and his corpse robbed, provoking Cole to join Quantrill intent on revenge. However, Cole also exhibited an idealism that separated him from the other guerillas, and he provided mercy to people during the war in some instances where Quantrill did not.

Cole Younger

By the second year of the war, Quantrill's band was blazing across western Missouri, chalking up success after success with its ruthless hit-and-run attacks. They hit Unionist civilians just as much as Union soldiers, incidentally gathering a fair amount of loot while striking a blow for the South.

Quantrill was a charismatic figure. He invented a story about how his brother had been murdered by Jayhawkers back in the 1850s. Quantrill said he hunted down every one of his brother's killed one by one and gruesomely enacted his vengeance. It was complete fabrication, but his comrades lapped it up. Regardless, he certainly proved himself as a natural guerrilla warrior. In a report dated February 3, 1862, Union Captain W.S. Oliver, stationed at Independence, wrote, "I have seen this infamous scoundrel rob mails, steal the coaches and horses, and commit other similar outrages upon society even within sight of this city. Mounted on the best horses of the country, he has defied pursuit. I hear of him tonight fifteen miles from here with new recruits, committing outrages on Union men, a large body of whom have come in tonight, driven out by him." Later that same month, Quantrill thumbed his nose at Oliver and his troops by riding right through Independence. While he was quickly driven out, that sort of panache appealed to young secessionists who felt Price and his underequipped army had abandoned them.

When Frank rode into Quantrill's camp, probably escorted by a friend already in the group, he would have had to tell of his experiences in Price's army and as a bushwhacker to prove his loyalty. He would have also needed to demonstrate his ability with a horse and gun. Then he had to answer the following questions: "Will you follow orders, be true to your fellows, and kill all those who serve and support the Union?" The correct answer to all of them, of course, was "yes", and Frank James proved good to his word. Frank remembered, "I will never forget the first time I saw Quantrill. He was nearly six feet in height, rather thin, his hair and moustache was sandy and he was full of life and a jolly fellow. He had none of the air of bravado or the desperado about him…he was a demon in battle."

Frank joined at the right time. Quantrill's group of raiders had grown to more than 100 or perhaps even as many as 200, and they were devastating western Missouri. The guerrilla war was turning even more gruesome, with soldiers shooting captured guerrillas and guerrillas mutilating the bodies of dead Union soldiers. Frank saw this group as his best chance at striking a serious blow against the Union forces in Missouri.

All the while, Union troops came down hard on local citizens suspected of being related to the guerrillas. Lieutenant Sardius Smith wrote in 1862, "We are getting quite hardened to this kind of thing and I can go into a house with a pistol in my hand, with a smile on my face, speak politely to the ladies, ask where their men are in order that I may shoot them or take them prisoner with as much grace as though I was making a call for friendship sake."

Quantrill's boldest strike came on August 21, 1863, when the raiders crossed the state line and attacked the nearly defenseless town of Lawrence, Kansas. The bushwhackers were incensed when a prison in Kansas City holding some of their female relatives collapsed, killing and wounding several. The Union command had thought that if they imprisoned the bushwhackers' womenfolk, the guerrillas might give up, but the plan backfired badly. Now the bushwhackers were out for blood and felt they rode on a righteous crusade of vengeance.

Though it's often forgotten now, the willingness of Quantrill's Raiders to conduct the risky raid on Lawrence, especially after many of them had continued their partisan activities without Quantrill's leadership, was not a foregone conclusion. Quantrill had to exercise considerable effort with his Confederate rank and popularity, and he knew that if he could not convince them to attack Lawrence now, he might never have the chance again. Eventually, his lieutenants - Anderson, Todd, Gregg, Cole Younger, and Yeager - unanimously agreed to destroy Lawrence and kill every male in the town. Gregg recalled, "He longed to get even with Kansas. His proposition was to go to Lawrence." He also later quoted what Quantrill said to the raiders: "The Kansan has been murdering and robbing our people for two years or more, and burned their houses by districts, hauled their household plunder, farming implements, etc., to Kansas, driven off their cattle, etc., until forbearance has ceased to be a virtue. Lawrence is the great hot-bed of abolitionism in Kansas. All the plunder (or at least the bulk of it) stolen from Missouri will be found stored away in Lawrence. We can get more revenge and more money there than anywhere else in the State of Kansas...I know the hazard this enterprise bears, but if you never risk, you never gain."

Most of the troops stationed at Lawrence were away hunting for bushwhackers, and in a hard night's riding, Quantrill led his men across the heavily guarded border region to hit the town at dawn. Lawrence had long been a hotbed of the antislavery movement and was home to Senator Jim Lane, a leading Jayhawker. Quantrill had made up a list of men to be killed, and Lane's name was right at the top.

While Quantrill fancied himself a soldier, his assault on Lawrence was anything but a military battle, and within the first hours of the sack, the raiders behaved just like partygoers who did not want to cease their celebrations. One of the participating raiders later wrote, "Demoniac yells rose above the crackling of pistol-shots. Hundreds of flags were secured from a book-store and tied to the tails of horses on which drunken guerrillas rode recklessly through the principal streets firing wildly and shouting in exultation for Quantrill, Jeff Davis, and the Southern Confederacy. Other bands bent on murder went about their business with method and dispatch. Victims were sought in homes, in shops, about the streets, in gardens, ravines, and fields of growing corn. Terror was carried to every heart. Women with disheveled and flowing hair clung desperately to husbands or brothers to shield them from the fury of the bushmen from beyond the border. Sometimes they were rudely flung aside with savage threats to save them injury from the bullet that bereaved them. When the deadly revolver was thrust between husband and wife she was deluged with blood following the muffled report that made her a widow. Fires were kindled in dwellings and shops and flames leaped and roared through all the streets and ways, consuming sometimes the living often the dead. Shrieks of distress and cries of despair could be heard above the uproar and tumult raging in the city. Hell was loosed and the pent wrath and mad fury nursed for years by border-ruffians against Lawrence ran bloody riot in the pandemonium of that awful day."

Although the raid on Lawrence had specific objectives, the discipline among Quantrill's Raiders inevitably began to break down. While bands led by Bloody Bill Anderson and Todd engaged in indiscriminate murder, other raiders intended to pillage the town for guns and liquor. Others were looking to steal horses and anything else they could use for making war. Quick work was made of the men who could fight, who were armed, and who posed a threat; the Union army barracks that still contained soldiers were mercilessly gutted by the raiders. Tents were knocked over, horses trampled over men still asleep, and others were shot. As the raiders descended on individual farms and homes, men were quickly led out of their houses at gunpoint.

By this time, most Lawrence inhabitants could read the writing on the wall. Some men begged for mercy and others tried to run, only to be shot down or executed in cold blood. Other husbands told their sons to run off so they could reason with the raiders, knowing full well that all they could ask was that the women and children be spared. One woman recalled a few weeks after the attack, "My father was very slow to get into the cornfield. He was so indignant at the ruffians that he was unwilling to retreat before them. My little children were in the field three hours. They seemed to know that if they cried the noise would betray their parents whereabouts, & so they kept as still as mice. The baby was very hungry & I gave her an ear of raw green corn which she ate ravenously." The raiders mostly obliged requests to spare women and children, but that decorum did not extend to their houses. Many families would have to spend the winter homeless.

By the time the raiders were done, some 200 men and boys lay dead and most of the town was in flames. Senator Lane managed to slip away and soon returned with a posse, only to find his house had been torched in his absence. Union cavalry detachments also converged on Lawrence, alerted by the huge column of billowing smoke. A grueling chase ensued, with the vengeful Unionists picking off stragglers. Most of Quantrill's men made it back to the safety of Missouri, and Frank James lived to fight on.

There has always been controversy over Frank's participation in the Lawrence Massacre because it doesn't fit in with his folk personality of the noble robber. There are no eyewitness accounts of his actions that day, but it is hard to believe he didn't leave without innocent blood on his hands. Frank himself never spoke of it.

Another raider and eventual partner in crime, Cole Younger, did speak of that terrible day. He had lost a relative in the Kansas City prison collapse and was unapologetic about his participation. He said, "It was a day of butchery. Bill Anderson claimed to have killed fourteen and the count was allowed. But it is not true that women were killed. One negro woman leaned out of a window and shouted: "You—of—." She toppled out dead before it was seen she was a woman. The death list that day is variously estimated at from 143 to 216 and the property loss by the firing of the town, the sacking of the bank, and the rest, at $1,500,000."

In fact, the Lawrence Massacre was so appalling that it even led to second-guessing by some of the raiders during the attack. One of the raiders explained, "Whatever can be said to the credit of any guerrilla in Lawrence should be set down. Not all of them were inhuman monsters, though many were. Even the worst were touched with pity sometimes and showed kindness. In many instances they offered to help remove furniture from buildings they fired. One bearded ruffian, bristling with deadly weapons, held the baby and entertained it by walking the floor and with "baby-talk" while Mrs. Fisher got him a lamp. Holding this babe touched his heart and he rode away at Mrs. Fisher's request to allow her to put out the fire he had helped to light. The building in which Mrs. Hoyt kept boarding-house was spared because she was a poor widow. General Holt protected H. S. Clarke and saved his life and dwelling. Because of the earnest pleading of the women, Doctor Griswold's house was not burned. George Todd protected the prisoners on the way from the Eldridge House to the City Hotel, and he saved the life of Arthur Spicer, whom Quantrill had before spared. Quantrill kept faith with the prisoners and protected them by a strong guard at the City Hotel, though it seemed at one time before they left the Eldridge House that he did not intend to keep his word with them. He listened to Stevens, his former attorney, and stood by his stipulation. Every guerrilla the author ever talked to said that there were men in the command which went to Lawrence who were opposed to going there at all and did not favor the purpose of the raid. Two showed their pistols, full-loaded and free of powder-soot to prove that they had not fired a shot and they expressed their purpose not to fire one in Lawrence."

Harper's Weekly illustrations depicting the ruins of Lawrence

Shocked at the violence of the raid, the Union command issued General Order Number Eleven, which removed virtually the entire civilian population from three western Missouri counties and a portion of another. These were hotbeds of secession and were used as bases for guerrilla activity. It was hoped that by denying the bushwhackers civilian support, they would go away. Union troops used the opportunity to loot and burn, and for more than a generation this region was known as the "Burnt District." Union Lieutenant-Colonel Bazel Lazear, who witnessed the clearance of civilians, wrote to his wife, "There are hundreds of people leaving their homes from this country and God knows what is to become of them. It is heart sickening to see what I have seen since I have been back here. A desolate country and women & children some of them almost naked. Some on foot and some in old wagons. Oh God what a sight to see in this once happy and peaceable country."

Lazear's pity did not extend to the men fighting for the South. In the same letter, he wrote, "There is no punishment on earth great enough for the villains who have brought this Rebellion about. I yesterday had one publically shot…He was in the Lawrence raid. He is the second prisoner I have had shot and I will have every one of them shot I can get a hold of, as such inhuman wretches deserve no mercy and should be shot down like dogs wherever found."

That winter, when Quantrill's group was wintering down in Texas, discipline fell apart. His men whooped it up in the little town of Sherman, riding their horses into shops and abusing the citizenry. The local Confederate commander tried to arrest some of the worst offenders but they always managed to escape or intimidate the regular soldiers. Quantrill, who had a commission as a captain from the Confederate government and fancied himself a regular soldier, tried to rein in his men, but to no avail.

Many of his men left him in favor of a new leader, a man who had participated gleefully in the Lawrence Massacre and yet disliked Quantrill for his pretensions of military leadership. This man was William Anderson, better known then and now as Bloody Bill. That winter he gathered some of the toughest of Quantrill's fighters around him. They would fight without Quantrill and his stifling discipline.

Quantrill rode back to Missouri with only 64 men, and lost most of them to the experienced bushwhacker George Todd, once his second-in-command. While Todd and Quantrill were playing poker, Todd drew a pistol and pointed it as his commander, asking if Quantrill was afraid of him. Quantrill had no choice but to say yes, losing face in front of his men. Todd and most of his men rode off, leaving Quantrill with almost no one.

Chapter 4: Jesse Joins the Fight

In the spring of 1864, when Frank James returned to Missouri in a small guerrilla group led by Fletch Taylor, Jesse James joined him. He was now 16, and no one was going to deny him a chance to take revenge on the Yankees. Sometime in late May, he met up with his brother, and Jesse would soon have his initiation into the harsh reality of guerrilla warfare. In early June, the group killed at least eight Unionist civilians and one slave, mostly by going up to their houses at night, dragging the man of family outside, and shooting him in front of his kinfolk. Then they would loot the house and leave.

The following month, Jesse experienced what might have been his first skirmish when the bushwhackers attacked the home of Solomon Bigelow, an early organizer of the Enrolled Missouri Militia who had since left the militia to return to his farm. While Bigelow was now a noncombatant, no one in those times could count themselves as neutral. When the bushwhackers attacked, Bigelow and his brother barricaded themselves inside and fired back. The brothers were eventually slain, but not before Jesse himself was slightly wounded. Some sources state that this was when he lost the tip of his finger, and that he hadn't shot it off himself as the popular legend goes.

The bushwhackers then ambushed a small Union patrol, and, buoyed by this success, joined with a Confederate recruiter who had gathered a few hundred local men. They rode to Platte City, where the local militia quickly changed sides. The hopeful rebels had heard rumors that Price was going to invade from Arkansas and decided they could hold the local area from the Union until he got there. Fletch Taylor thought otherwise and soon left with his bushwhacker band, but not before killing an abolitionist minister. The retreat was a wise move, because the Union troops arrived in force, quickly scattered the Platte City rebels, and burned the town.

With Union troops scouring the countryside, Fletch Taylor and his men broke into small groups to elude pursuit. Frank and Jesse decided to move on and find a new leader, and they soon found one in Frank's old comrade, Bloody Bill Anderson. As violent as Anderson already was, when one of his sisters died in the Kansas City prison collapse, it appears he went insane. He'd often ride into battle foaming at the mouth, shouting out his sister's name. Jim Cummins, a bushwhacker from Clay County, wrote of Anderson, "You talk about Quantrill, Todd, and Taylor being reckless raiders and fighters, but Anderson I thought was worse than any of them when I joined him."

Despite this, Anderson was now leading the majority of Quantrill's old force in a raid across western Missouri, leaving a trail of scalped bodies and burning homes in his wake. While bloodthirsty and perhaps a bit crazy, Anderson was a wise leader. Frank recalled how he made sure everyone kept their horses, guns, and equipment in good condition, and his battles with the enemy generally showed good tactical sense.

That August, Bloody Bill made it to Clay County, which had not been included in General Order Number Eleven. Local secessionists cheered him, and Zerelda fed Anderson and his men as they camped in her backyard. Frank and Jesse were hailed as local heroes. Of course, the Union troops in Clay County thought otherwise. As they gathered their forces, Anderson decided to move east into Ray County. He made short work of two EMM patrols and picked off several lone civilians, during which Anderson and his men often scalped their victims and tied the grisly trophies to their saddles.

At least one contemporary source notes that Jesse participated in this, and it would be hard to imagine he wouldn't. He was one of the newest and youngest of the group, and given that he was fatherless and humiliated by Union troops, he would have wanted to impress the older men of the band as much as he wanted to get his own revenge against the enemy. He had joined an elite brotherhood of warriors, riding on the best horses, each armed with several pistols, and making bold charges and ambushes at the hated Union foe. Frank, too, mostly likely participated in the scalpings and murders.

In mid-August, the group passed a farm and Jesse spotted a saddle sitting on a fence outside a home. It was much better than the one he was using, so he decided, in typical bushwhacker fashion, to take it. Just then the farmer came out the front door and shot him in the chest. The man got away as the bushwhackers took the stricken boy to the home of a local secessionist, who hid him in the attic. If the soldiers found him, both Jesse and the farmer would surely be killed.

Reluctantly Frank rode out with the rest of the bushwhackers, wondering if he would ever see his brother again.

Chapter 5: A Bloody Ride across Missouri

By the summer of 1864, the Confederate cause west of the Mississippi had become truly desperate. The rebels had lost Missouri, northern Arkansas, the Indian Territory, and strips of coastline along Western Louisiana and Texas. The Trans-Mississippi Department, under the command of Major-General Kirby Smith, still boasted some 60,000 troops on paper, but in reality only a fraction could be put into the field. Some were tied up in western Texas skirmishing with Union cavalry and Native Americans, while others guarded the fronts in Arkansas and Louisiana or hid along the western bank of the Mississippi keeping an eye on Union gunboats. Thousands were scattered over a vast area protecting civilians against bandits or trying to guard the region's creaking infrastructure. They were underfed, underarmed, and low on morale, with their ranks hemorrhaging from desertions and disease.

Something had to be done before the department collapsed under the weight of its own despair. Taking advantage of the glimmer of hope sparked by pushing back a pair of ill-planned Union offensives up the Red River and into central Arkansas in the spring of 1864, General Sterling Price renewed his call for a campaign to retake Missouri, and this time Kirby Smith decided to listen. While he harbored doubts about Price's promises to take St. Louis, he did think some action would be better than none, and he was under pressure from Richmond to act in some way in order to distract Union attention and divert men from the campaigns east of the river. He also reasoned that with the U.S. presidential election coming up, an invasion of Missouri might tip the vote in favor of George B. McClellan, who was running against Lincoln and was hinting at making peace with the Confederacy.

Thus, Price gathered 12,000 men to invade Missouri. They varied from veterans to all-but-useless deserters he had rounded up. Some rode fine horses and wielded the best weaponry, while others had no mounts or weapons at all. Price had gathered simply everyone he could in order to launch his offensive. Missouri bushwhackers would play an integral part in Price's strategy. He called on them to weaken Union resistance ahead of his arrival by destroying infrastructure and hitting isolated outposts. The idea was a sound one. Price's greatest fear was that the Union garrisons would be able to join forces before he could take St. Louis or his secondary objective of the state capital at Jefferson City. By cutting telegraph wires, burning bridges, and keeping Union troops holed up in their blockhouses, Price would be able to move further into Missouri before being noticed.

While Price's initial strategy was sound, he ruined his chances of making a lightning thrust into the state by bringing along, in addition to his cavalry, a large number of infantry and a lumbering wagon train. Riding with him was a small secondary army of politicians and speculators who came along to take over Missouri once the Yankees had been evicted, including Thomas Reynolds, now Confederate Governor of Missouri after the death of Claiborne Fox Jackson. Price, having decided on a quick cavalry campaign, had gone back to his old thinking that all the Missouri population would rise up to help him.

Price wasted even more time trying to take Fort Davidson, in the lead-rich Arcadia Valley in southeastern Missouri. Price hoped to capture the large supply of weapons and ammunition stored there, which he sorely needed. On September 27, he launched a massive assault on the earthworks, only to watch his men get cut down by a hail of musket fire. The fort's cannons gouged bloody paths through regiment after regiment. Those who made it to the earthworks got trapped in a deep ditch, where they got blown to pieces by crude grenades. At last the rebels retreated, having lost more than a thousand men. That night the Union defenders managed to slip away and blow up the fort with a slow-burning fuse. Price then chased the fort's defenders for three days, wasting even more time and not even managing to capture them.

Frustrated, Price ordered his army north. Scouts told him St. Louis was already receiving reinforcements thanks to his fruitless attack on Fort Davidson, so he decided not to risk attacking the city. Instead, the army moved west, heading for the state capital at Jefferson City. As the army moved along, Price stopped to give speeches and gain recruits. He seemed to have lost all sense of haste, instead reveling in the cheers of local secessionists who brought their rebel flags out of hiding at the approach of his army.

By the time he got to Jefferson City, he found it well fortified and garrisoned with large numbers of reinforcements. Once again he decided to move on; the slaughter at Fort Davidson was still fresh in his memory. Governor Reynolds and the other politicians objected, but not too loudly. Indeed, they had already started losing hope as they saw the "invasion" slowly turn into a farce.

In fact, the farce was about to turn deadly. While Price had won a series of skirmishes against small local Union garrisons, a Union army numbering 14,000 men was moving out of St. Louis in pursuit. Kansas was also on the alert and was gathering an equally large force.

When Bloody Bill Anderson received Price's order to soften up Union resistance before the invasion, he was camped with about 250 men in Boone County, along the Missouri River in the center of the state. Jesse James had just returned, having recovered from his wound, which turned out not to have been as dangerous as it at first appeared. Anderson joined up with the guerrilla group of George Todd, which included Quantrill and his small following. On September 24, they rode into the town of Fayette wearing Union uniforms.

At first the townspeople and garrison were fooled, but then one of the bushwhackers saw a black man in a Union uniform and shot at him. Their cover blown, the bushwhackers went wild, spreading through town and setting off their pistols. Most of the troops managed to retreat to a wooden blockhouse. Safely behind the log walls, they held off a brave but foolish charge that left several bushwhackers writhing on the ground in pools of their own blood. Frank James later remembered, "It was like charging a stone wall, only this stone wall belched forth lead."

Under a heavy fire, Frank, Jesse, and two other bushwhackers managed to grab two of their wounded comrades and take them to safety. Frank quipped, "I tell you, pride makes most of us do many things we wouldn't otherwise...Well, pride kept us there until we got [the wounded] rolled up in a blanket and then we made tracks." The guerrillas had lost 13 dead and at least 30 wounded, while killing only one or two soldiers.

Next, Anderson decided to hit the railroad town of Centralia, population approximately 100. At dawn on September 27th, Anderson rode into town with 80 men, including Frank and Jesse, yelling and shooting their pistols to terrify the inhabitants into submission. Anderson wanted to read the St. Louis newspapers for information on Price's movements, and he didn't mind that his men set about plundering the town's two stores and approximately 20 homes. Letting the boys cut loose was good for morale, especially after the humiliating defeat at Fayette. Someone found a keg of whiskey and several guerrillas got drunk and set fire to the train depot. Another bushwhacker discovered crates of boots and everyone helped themselves to new footwear.

As Anderson's men ran wild, bursting into homes to demand breakfast and robbing people at gunpoint, a stagecoach from the county seat, Columbia, drew into town. The guerrillas hauled out all the passengers, including U.S. Rep. James Rollins, and proceeded to rob them. A guerrilla shoved a pistol into the politician's face and demanded to know his name. The quick-thinking Unionist sputtered out, "The Reverend Mr. Johnson, minister of the Methodist Church, South." The drunken guerrilla didn't wonder why this supposed preacher would refer to himself as "Mr. Johnson," and merely got busy rifling through his valise, eyes gleaming as he tried on the congressman's silk shirt. Rollins' heart must have thundered in his chest when he realized his initials were monogrammed on the breast pocket, but the guerrilla didn't notice.

Rollins

At 11:35 a.m., the westbound train from St. Charles pulled in, carrying 23 unarmed Union soldiers on furlough or medical leave. Among them was Sgt. Thomas Goodman of the First Missouri Engineers. He was part of Sherman's army and was enjoying a 30 day furlough. Heading back to his wife and children in Iowa, he must have been eagerly anticipating the end of the last leg of his journey, but his daydreams of kissing his wife and playing with his children were shattered along with the windows of the train as bullets flew through them. "In a moment more we were inside a line of blazing murderous weapons," he remembered, "and volley after volley was poured into the train until we came to a dead stop." The guerrillas burst inside, ordering all the passengers out of the train. Goodman recalled some of them saying that if they surrendered quietly, they would be treated as prisoners of war. The guerrillas lined them up and stripped them of their uniforms. Goodman and most of the others stood helpless in their underwear, while some stood completely naked. More bushwhackers lined up opposite the prisoners and covered them with their pistols.

Then Bloody Bill Anderson stepped forward and surveyed the Union troops, his cold eyes ranging up and down the column. Goodman described him as a "pale, sad looking man" about 5'10 tall and "round and compact in form, slender in person, quick and lithe in action as a tiger—whose nature at times he possessed. His complexion naturally was soft and very fair, but had taken a tinge of brown from his exposed manner of life." Anderson's dark brown hair "hung in thick, clustering masses about his head and neck." His eyes "were a strange mixture of blue and gray…cold, unsympathizing, and expressionless…"

Those eyes surveyed the line. "Boys, have you a sergeant in your ranks?" he asked. This question was met with profound silence. But then Goodman noticed one of the guerrillas examining his stolen uniform. On the cuff were the three chevrons denoting the rank of sergeant. The man looked at the uniform, looked at Goodman and, apparently remembering who he took it from, walked toward Anderson.

Goodman feared what would happen if he was caught in a lie, so he meekly stepped forward and admitted he was a sergeant. Anderson ordered him to stand aside. Goodman thought he was a dead man, but to his surprise Anderson gave the order to "muster out" the privates. The bushwhackers opened fire, emptying their revolvers into the prisoners. As the smoke cleared, Goodman saw his comrades lying dead or dying on the ground. A few crawled along in the dirt, leaving bloody trails behind them until a guerrilla shot them in the head. One soldier, Sergeant Val Peters, a big bear of a man who had lost even his underwear to the guerrillas, decided to fight to the death. He charged the guerrilla line, bullet after bullet tearing through his flesh, and pummeled several men with his giant fists. Then he managed to dive under the train platform, but the rebels surrounded the platform and set fire to it. As thick black smoke curled into his hideout, Peters sprinted out from under the blazing planks wielding a piece of firewood. Again he charged into a storm of bullets, smacking two of the guerrillas to the ground before falling dead, more than 20 slugs riddling his body.

It was all over in a couple of minutes, but the horror was just beginning for Sergeant Goodman. "The guerrillas, with horrid oaths and wild fierce looks, gloated over the bodies of the slain, or spurned them from their path with brutal violence," he later wrote. Instead, the guerrillas took out their aggression on the train, looting $10,000 from the registered mail and giving the James boys a lesson in the profitability of robbing trains. Then the bushwhackers set it on fire and sent it off down the line. The billowing column of smoke from the blazing locomotive could be seen for miles, but the flaming train did no damage because the engineer had tied the whistle down so the train ran out of steam and soon came to a halt. Putting Goodman on a mule and flanking him with guards, Anderson's men set off toward the main group back at camp. Some were considerate enough to use the stolen boots to carry some of the liberated whiskey back to their friends in camp.

At 4:00 p.m., Union Major A.V.E. Johnston led 148 mounted riflemen from the 39th Missouri

Infantry into Centralia. He had been hunting the guerrillas since the previous day and had seen the smoke from the burning train. Despite being unsure of the enemy numbers, Johnson divided his force, leaving some to restore order in town while he led 115 men in pursuit. A mile outside of Centralia he saw 10 riders galloping away from him. They were a ruse designed to draw Johnson into an ambush, and they did their job perfectly. The Union men followed them for a couple of miles before riding over a low rise of open prairie and seeing a line of guerrillas at the bottom of the slope. Each rebel stood by his horse, one foot on the ground and one in the stirrup. More were hidden in the woods to either side.

Johnson's mounted infantry carried single-shot Enfield rifles that were difficult to fire and almost impossible to reload on horseback, so he ordered them to dismount and form a line. The bushwhackers swung into their saddles and drew their revolvers. Those to the flanks appeared out of the tree line to join their comrades. Johnston gave the order to fire but his volley went high, a common mistake for inexperienced men shooting downhill. The 39th had just been recruited a few weeks before. Only three guerrillas dropped from their saddles, one splashing his brains on Frank James' boot, and within moments the guerrillas smashed through the Union line, slaughtering them with repeated shots from their Colt revolvers. Frank James remembered the blue-clad troops frantically trying to reload or fix bayonets while falling under a withering close-range fire. Jesse ducked several shots from Maj. Johnston before shooting him down.

Once more, a slaughter ensued. "Men's heads were severed from their lifeless bodies, exchanged as to bodies, labeled with rough and obscene epitaphs in inscriptions, stuck upon their carbine points, tied to their saddle bows, or sat grinning at each other from the tops of fence stakes and stumps around the scene," Goodman recalled.

With most of the Union detachment dead and the rest fleeing in panic, the guerrillas galloped back into Centralia and made short work of the other part of Johnston's command. The 39th lost 114 men and two officers killed, two wounded, and six missing that day. The low number of wounded was due to Anderson's "no quarter" policy. There was a law in Missouri that any guerrilla caught would be put to death, and Bloody Bill saw no reason why he shouldn't reciprocate.

The guerrilla leader had won a great victory, but now he had to escape. Soon the countryside would be alive with bluecoats. He scattered his men, taking Goodman with him, and these small groups traveled in all directions through the countryside they knew so well, keeping to the old deer trails and little-used back roads. Throughout his ordeal Goodman took careful note of everything that occurred in camp, and his memoir is the only document by a Union soldier of life among the bushwhackers.

After a hard ride, portions of Anderson's band regrouped at a remote thicket. Goodman described the scene: "From the evidences to be noted around, this spot had served them as a camp or general rendezvous for some time past, and rough shelters had been constructed of poles, bark and boughs, presenting a rude but very fitting attribute of their way of life. They seemed to possess some sort of a depository or commissary establishment here, and both 'grub and whiskey' were dispensed, with a very liberal hand. The consequence might be easily foreseen. By night nearly the whole command, Anderson and Todd included, were drunk even to madness. God help me, I never witnessed so much profanity in the same space of time as before, nor since; and it is my earnest desire, I never may again. They whooped, ran, jumped and yelled like so many savages. Once, Anderson, leaping on a horse, rode wildly through the crowd; firing his revolvers indiscriminately, and yelling like one possessed."

Anderson rendezvoused with the rest of his men at the Missouri River several days later, near the steamboat port town of Rocheport, or at least where Rocheport used to be; the entire town had been burned by Federal troops in retaliation for its strong Southern sympathies. The remaining locals, their Southern spirit undiminished, hid some boats in the brush along the river so the guerrillas could get to the south bank. As the men gathered by the river that night, Goodman managed to slip away into the darkness and escape.

Meanwhile, General Price led his army west from Jefferson City, where on October 11 at the Missouri River port of Boonville he held a big rally for the local secessionists while his men looted Unionist homes and shops. Bloody Bill's group rode into town. These tough riders, each packing several revolvers and galloping around on swift steeds while wearing brightly decorated shirts from their female kinfolk or sweethearts, made a marked contrast to Price's ragged men. Moreover, General Price and Governor Reynolds were shocked and enraged when they noticed the scalps dangling from the bushwhackers' saddles, and they demanded that the bushwhackers remove them. The bushwhackers departed, did as they were told, and came back. Price seemed to have forgotten the incident and gracefully accepted a pair of silver-plated pistols as a gift from Anderson. He then ordered Anderson to cross to the north side of the river and destroy the North Missouri Railroad.

As it turned out, the general would never see the famed guerrilla leader again. Price headed west towards Kansas City, pushing an increasingly large force of Union troops ahead of him while the Union army from St. Louis began to close in to his rear. They caught up with him on October 23 at the town of Westport, close to the Kansas state line. In front of him Price saw a large army of Kansans. He was trapped, and the battle was a disaster. While Price was able to break out, he lost some 1,500 men. Another bad defeat came at Mine Creek two days later, where Price lost one of his generals, 1,200 more men, and nearly all his artillery. His army shattered, he fled all the way back to Arkansas, his men freezing, starving, and deserting along the way.

Meanwhile, Anderson and his men continued attacking Union civilians and the occasional Union patrol, but besides burning a couple of depots, they never attacked the railroad they had been ordered to destroy. Instead, they doubled back and followed Price's army as it moved towards disaster at Westport. Being on the north side of the river while all the action was going on to the south, they thought they had the citizenry at their mercy. They looted and murdered at will, although on October 20 they got bushwhacked themselves when a plucky detachment of the EMM hit them in their camp early one morning. Frank and Jesse fought a rearguard action that allowed the rest of the band to escape.

A few days later, the group, which had now split up and only numbered some 80 men, made it back to the James farm to enjoy some of Zerelda's home cooking. Then they rode out again for more looting of civilians and skirmishing with Union militia. This time, however, Bloody Bill's luck ran out. On October 27, while riding through Ray County, he came across a detachment of the EMM under Lieutenant-Colonel Samuel P. Cox. This wily Union officer turned the tables on the bushwhackers by employing one of their own tactics against them. Having heard where Anderson was bivouacked, he sent a detachment to fire into their camp and ride off. Anderson took the bait and followed in hot pursuit with some of his men, including Jesse James, but the attack had been a ruse. The attackers led the bushwhackers into an ambush, during which Anderson and several others fell dead.

Chapter 6: A Final Gamble

With General Price's army gone, the rebels in Missouri began to lose hope. Once again it was up to the bushwhackers to carry on the fight. Now, however, their numbers were fewer, whittled down to a hard core that included some men who were nothing more than opportunists and bandits. The more experienced bands fled to Texas for their usual winter antics, and Missouri's thick foliage thinned out in winter, making it harder to hide. For those reasons, the bushwhackers had made it their habit to leave the state until springtime, including Jesse.

For his part, Frank chose another path. In December he joined with Quantrill on an ambitious new raid into Kentucky. Later reports claim Quantrill was heading for Washington, D.C. in order to assassinate Abraham Lincoln, but it's more likely he simply wanted to get out of the region where he was known too well and hunted too diligently.

It seems surprising that the brothers would split after riding through so many tough fights together, but they always showed a willingness to go their separate ways from time to time. Like other such separations throughout their lives, it remains unclear why they split up. Perhaps Jesse preferred to stick with Anderson's old gang, or perhaps he thought the war was coming to an end and wanted to stay close to familiar faces and places instead of riding off into Kentucky with a leader he didn't know well. Whatever the reason, there didn't seem to be any hard feelings.

Back on the James farm, Reuben and Zerelda finally faced the consequences of harboring the guerrillas. They and a few other rebel families were banished from the state. The couple stocked up a wagon and left for Nebraska in January of 1865.

Jesse wintered in Sherman, Texas. He must have fumed at the thought of his mother and father-in-law being sent into exile if he had heard, but he needed no further motivation to continue the fight. He joined the gang of Archie Clement, an old comrade from Anderson's group who many veteran bushwhackers recalled as the brains of the outfit. In April, Clement led about 70 bushwhackers back into Missouri. They heard of Lee's surrender at Appomattox, but they dismissed it as "a damned Yankee lie."

Clement

The bushwhackers scalped a militiaman on the banks of the Osage River, looted the village of Holden and killed a civilian there. They also did the same to eight more civilians in nearby Kingville, and they sent a note to the commander at Lexington demanding his surrender. This was ignored; the Confederacy was no more, and many bushwhackers had not returned from Texas. In early May, some started turning themselves in. When they weren't lynched, more rode out of the brush to join them.

Clement decided to give up too. He sent a note suggesting a meeting to discuss terms on May 17, but the parlay never came off. On May 15, the group stumbled upon a Union patrol. In the ensuing firefight, Jesse fell out of the saddle with a bullet through his lung. He staggered into the woods and hid out near a creek. "I lay in the water all night," he recalled. "I felt as if I was burning up. The next morning, I crawled up the bank and there was a man plowing who helped me get to my friends...I was in a dreadful fix...everybody thought the wound would be mortal."

Jesse later garnished the story by saying he was riding into town to surrender, but the historical record and Clement's own letter to the commander at Lexington show that the proposed meeting was still two days away.

The fight didn't stop the bushwhackers' surrender but only delayed it. On May 21, the distraught bushwhackers rode into Lexington, carrying Jesse James with them so they could take the oath of allegiance. His cousin Zee nursed him back to health, and as he lay recovering he proposed to her. At first they kept their engagement a secret, fearing their relatives wouldn't approve.

Meanwhile, Quantrill led his gang on a long ride into Kentucky, following the usual bushwhacker tactics of cutting telegraph wires and skirmishing with patrols while confusing civilians with their Union uniforms. They caused little serious damage, however, because in that state the rebellion had all but died and they could find no support. Quantrill was mortally wounded on May 10 in a skirmish with a patrol sent out to hunt for him. While the remnants of his band continued their hit-and-run fighting, they must have seen it was hopeless. Frank gave up on July 26, 1865, took an oath of loyalty to the United States, and went home.

Chapter 7: Outlaws

After the war ended, former guerrillas were mostly able to return to their civilian homes and jobs and get on with their lives. All was not well, however. A new state constitution in Missouri barred former relatives from holding public office or working a variety of jobs such as lawyers, teachers, or preachers. They were also barred from voting, thus guaranteeing that the Republican Party would dominate state politics. The former rebels rankled under these restrictions but there was little they could do but complain.

Like so many veterans, Frank and Jesse had a hard time readjusting to civilian life. They had seen too much, done too much, and hated too deeply. Their feelings weren't helped by the attitude of the state government, run by the so-called Radical Republicans, which banned all former Confederates from voting, holding public office, preaching, practicing law, and several other professions. Confederates who had not paid taxes during the war often came home to find their farms had been seized and sold to Unionists. Some became the victims of revenge killings.

In reality, the James family got off relatively easy. Reuben and Zerelda returned from exile in August of 1865. They had kept their land, and their slaves, now free, continued to work on the farm as many former slaves did. Faced with few opportunities and nowhere to go, slaves often chose to stay in their familiar surroundings. The farm in Clay County remained a prosperous one, and there is no record of Frank and Jesse being persecuted.

Nonetheless, the war had hardened them. They had become accustomed to the life of saddle and gun, and tilling the soil paled in comparison, especially for fiery young Jesse, who was always the more rambunctious of the two.

There has been much speculation about the inner workings of the James-Younger gang that became the most notorious group of outlaws in the wake of the war. The group was a fluid one, with members coming and going and different jobs requiring larger or smaller numbers of men. It's also unclear who was in charge. Since these were independent-minded criminals and former guerrillas, much was probably done on consensus, with Frank James and Cole Younger as the leading thinkers. After all, they were older and had the most war experience. Jesse James was certainly the most outspoken member of the group. He was constantly sending letters to the press proclaiming his innocence and stating that he would appear in court if he thought he could get a fair trial, but it appears to have been his older and more level-headed brother Frank, along with Cole Younger, who made most of the decisions. One member of the gang, George Shepard, who was captured shortly after the robbery of the Southern Bank of Kentucky on March 21, 1868, said in a newspaper interview, "Frank is the most shrewd, cunning, and capable; in fact, Jesse can't compare with him. Frank is a man of education, and can act the fine gentleman on all occasions. Jesse is reckless, and a regular dare-devil in courage, but it's Frank makes who all the plans and perfects the methods of escape. Jesse is a fighter and that's all. . .[Frank] would rather not be known, so he directs Jesse and Jesse directs the crowd. He [Jesse] likes notoriety and always takes care to let the people on trains know that he is the leader, and he always enjoyed the reading of his exploits in the papers."

Cole Younger

Jim Younger

John Younger

Bob Younger

The secretive and mercurial nature of the gang allowed members to claim innocence of individual crimes even when they were implicated as being part of the group. In his autobiography, Cole wrote that "right here I want to state, and I will take my oath solemnly that what I say is the truth, and *nothing but the truth, notwithstanding all the accusations that have been made against me, I never, in all my life, had anything whatever to do with robbing any bank in the state of Missouri.* I could prove that I was not in the towns where banks were robbed in Missouri, at the time that the raids took place, and in many instances that I was thousands of miles away."

This simply wasn't true. Eyewitness accounts and testimony from captured outlaws put the

Younger brothers at numerous holdups. Younger wrote his autobiography after getting out of prison and returning to Missouri; he was obviously trying to stave off any hostility from the people of his home state.

Less than a year after the end of the war, a group of former bushwhackers decided to go on another raid, but this time, instead of fighting for the South, they would be fighting for their own gain. On February 13, 1866, about a dozen men rode into Liberty, Missouri. Three stayed outside of town to act as sentries while the rest, some of whom wore false beads and wigs, rode up to the Clay County Savings Association Bank. Two entered the bank, pulled pistols on the two employees inside, and cleared out the vault of $57,000 in cash, gold, and Federal notes. They then closed the two men inside and hurried off to their horses. What they didn't realize, however, was that they hadn't locked the vault, and within a few moments the bank workers were screaming out the window that they'd been robbed. The gang galloped out of town, firing their guns to intimidate passersby, and one local university student, in the wrong place at the wrong time, caught a fatal bullet.

The Clay County Savings Bank

The theft has gone down in history as America's first daytime bank robbery in peacetime and the first adventure of what would become known as the James-Younger gang. There have been various theories as to who made up the group that day, but most lawmen at the time, and later historians, agree that Frank James was in on it, as well as many veterans of Quantrill's raiders and Bloody Bill Anderson's outfits. Jesse James is often said to have rode with the gang, but he was still recovering from the gunshot wound he received late in the war, so this seems unlikely. Historians still dispute whether Cole Younger was among the robbers.

More robberies followed, and it appears Jesse had a hand in these because in September of 1869, he requested to have his membership to the Mount Olive Baptist Church canceled "for the stated reason that he believed himself unworthy." That said, there was no clear connection made between a bank robbery and Jesse James until December 7, 1869. Jesse and the other robbers were looking for Samuel P. Cox, a member of the Union militia that killed Bill Anderson. Jesse and another man – most likely Frank - went to Gallatin, Missouri and robbed the Daviess County Savings Association after asking for small bills in exchange for a $100 bill. During the robbery, respected community citizen and family man Captain John W. Sheets was fatally shot in the heart and head. Sheets was working as the bank's cashier, and Jesse mistakenly believed that Sheets was Cox, so he murdered Sheets on the spot while getting away with less than $1,000. The robbers subsequently boasted that they had killed Major Samuel P. Cox, and while it was a case of mistaken identity, it is significant that they were justifying their robbery by settling an old score.

Naturally, Jesse's boasts about killing Cox had the effect of implicating him in the robbery and murder, and Gallatin was in an uproar. The governor of Missouri offered a reward for the capture of Jesse and Frank, and the *St. Joseph Gazette* provided details of the robbery and murder. Mentioning Jesse and Frank by name as the suspects, the article marked the first time that Jesse's name appeared in print in connection to a crime. It was exactly what Jesse had been waiting for. For a man who spent much of his brief life seeking attention, he had it now, and with the help of a newspaperman from Kansas City, Jesse James would soon become a household name.

John Newman Edwards was a former officer in the Confederate army who worked as an editor at the *Kansas City Times*. An alcoholic who was still bitter over the war, he was eager to stir up the former Confederates within the Democratic Party. His interests were purely political, as he wanted the ex-Confederates to resume their place of power. He saw the story in the *Gazette* about Jesse and Frank James and, with it, an opportunity to spread propaganda about the former Confederates of the Civil War, which in turn could potentially help his cause. He had already shown no hesitancy to portray armed rebels as victims of radicals from the North.

Edwards

Edwards met with Frank and Jesse and quickly realized that Jesse sought the limelight far more than Frank did. Jesse possessed almost an urgency to be noticed and this played well into Edwards' desire to create a story about the unfair treatment of ex-Confederates. About six months after the robbery in Gallatin, Jesse wrote an open letter to the governor, which Edwards printed in the *Times*. Jesse claimed that he was innocent of the charges against him and that the Union men were the true criminals. Jesse said that he was being unfairly cast as an outlaw simply because he held beliefs that were different from the Union. The creation of the mythical Jesse James was underway.

It was Edwards who started the myth that Jesse was the modern day Robin Hood who stole from the rich to give to the poor. In 1873, he devoted 20 pages to the James gang, glorifying their achievements as noble and for the greater good. Jesse was so enamored with the image that Edwards would create for him that he named his son, Jesse Edward James, after Edwards, although Jesse, Jr. was known as Tim. To make sure there was no doubt that he had been there, Jesse even took to leaving press releases at his crime scenes. He had no difficulty trying to live up to the image Edwards created, usually dressing in style and carrying a Bible that looked like it had been referred to often.

The James and Younger brothers moved freely about their home turf in Missouri, and thanks to Edwards, the public was convinced that the gang was on a noble pursuit. Not only did state residents refuse to turn the gang in, they helped shield them from the law, making the task of finding the gang very difficult for Missouri authorities. This coincided with ex-Confederates winning back their seats in the state Senate. The conditions were ripe for the mythical Jesse to flourish.

That said, Edwards had a tough job, because the string of robberies performed by the gang victimized Southerners as well as Northerners. At times they would spare Confederate veterans and working men, although more often these people were robbed too, so it appears this preference was a matter of whim.

In the next few years the gang seemed to be everywhere, hitting banks and stagecoaches in Missouri and Arkansas. Jesse James got into the habit of writing letters to the papers proclaiming his innocence while at the same time saying he was a fugitive because of Yankee persecution. Of course, as the gang's fame spread, so did their supposed robberies; they were only one of many gangs riding the countryside committing robberies, but most crimes were laid at their door.

On June 3, 1871, the gang was certainly involved in a job up in Iowa. Cole Younger, Clell Miller, and Frank and Jesse James robbed the Obocock Brothers bank of Corydon of $6,000. This time the heist was better planned. Most of the town was in the yard of the local Methodist church listening to a politician speak, but while the bandits had gotten away with no gunplay, they couldn't resist a bit of showmanship. One of the robbers rode up and announced to the crowd that the bank had been robbed. Everyone figured he was a heckler and ignored him, only to find out later he had been speaking the truth.

That crime brought additional attention to Jesse James, and it was an indication that James and his gang were operating across multiple states. In fact, the gang would operate as far south as Texas and as far east as West Virginia. Powerless to stop outlaws like James, banks began turning to the Pinkerton Detective Agency in an attempt to track them down. In the 1850s, Allan Pinkerton had established a private detective and security guard agency in Chicago, a forerunner of sorts for both private investigators and the Secret Service. A decade later, the Pinkertons, as the agency was informally called, claimed to have uncovered and thwarted a plan to assassinate President Abraham Lincoln, and from there they created the first secret service in the U.S. during the Civil War. In an effort to fight back against the notorious outlaws that targeted the nation's railroad system, railroad companies such as Union Pacific hired the Pinkertons to join forces with their own police force to capture the outlaws that preyed on their trains. Now the banks were getting in on the act and hiring the Pinkertons to protect them as well.

Allan Pinkerton

As it turned out, the Pinkerton connection would be the undoing of the James-Younger gang. They had been in the habit of focusing their work in their home state of Missouri, but with various posses and Pinkerton detectives on their tail, decided to ride all the way to Minnesota to rob a bank there. In September of 1876, they settled on robbing a bank in Northfield. Cole Younger explained, "Gen. Benjamin F. Butler, whom we preferred to call 'Silver Spoons' Butler from his New Orleans experiences during the war, had a lot of money invested, we were told, in the First National Bank at Northfield, Minnesota, as also had J. T. Ames, Butler's son-in-law, who had been the "carpet-bag" governor of Mississippi after the war. Butler's treatment of the Southerners during the war was not such as to commend him to our regard, and we felt little compunction, under the circumstances, about raiding him or his."

Butler had been the Union commander over New Orleans for part of the war, running an infamously corrupt administration. His son-in-law, Ames, was a Union commander, so it made sense for the gang, which out of nine members included five ex-bushwhackers, to target the First National Bank. Their movements before the robbery, however, indicate they cased many banks before choosing the one at Northfield, which means the Union connection to the bank was of secondary importance, perhaps seen by the gang only as a bonus to the large amounts of cash they hoped to steal.

Whatever their initial plans were, after they took a look at Northfield they decided this to be their target and set the date of the robbery as September 7. On that day, they rode into town in two separate groups, stopping at separate restaurants to eat an early lunch. Cole recounted that things went badly from the start: "Between the time we broke camp and the time they reached the bridge the three who went ahead [Bob Younger, Charlie Pitts, and Frank James] drank a quart of whisky, and there was the initial blunder at Northfield. I never knew Bob to drink before, and I did not know he was drinking that day till after it was all over."

While Bob and Charlie were relatively inexperienced and probably nervous, it's surprising that one of the James brothers would drink before the job. By 2:00 p.m., the carousing was over and the gang rode across a bridge and into the town square where the bank was located. They immediately attracted attention, and some of the citizens began to wonder about these strange newcomers. The first to arrive were Pitts, Bob Younger, and Frank James. They hitched their horses in front of the bank and entered just as Cole Younger and Clell Miller rode up. Jim Younger, Jesse James, and Bill Stiles were taking up the rear.

Younger recalled, "When Miller and myself crossed over the bridge, I saw a crowd of citizens about the corners, also our boys sitting there on some boxes. I remarked to Miller about the crowd and said, 'Surely the boys will not go into the bank with so many people about. I wonder why they did not ride straight through the town.' We were half way across the square when we saw the three men rise and walk up the sidewalk towards the bank. Miller said: 'They are going in,' and I replied, 'If they do the alarm will be given as sure as there's a hell.'"

The bridge and town square

Out on the street, two men grew suspicious of Cole and Clell. J.S. Allen, owner of a hardware and gun store in town, walked toward the bank, but Clell grabbed him to stop him from going inside. Allen could see through the window that the bank was being robbed, and even though Clell told him to keep quiet as he shoved him away from the bank, Allen yelled out that the bank was being robbed and told anyone within earshot to grab a gun. Henry Wheeler, a medical student home from college on a break, joined in and began shouting a warning that their bank was being robbed. Clell shot at Wheeler and just missed shooting him in the head.

Now that the game was up, the five outlaws outside the bank sprang into their saddles and started to clear the streets. They rode up and down, firing at anyone in sight and shouting for them to get away. However, if this was supposed to scare the citizens of Northfield, it didn't work. Instead, the locals grabbed guns and started firing back from around corners or from upper windows. Three civilians even posted themselves at a nearby street corner and threw rocks.

Within moments, the bandits were in trouble. Clell Miller took a load of birdshot to the face and fell off his horse. Miller staggered to his feet, remounted, and then took a fatal rifle bullet in the chest. As Cole rushed to help him, he got a bullet in the hip. Pitts' horse was also killed, and Stiles fell with a bullet through the heart. Every one of the robbers outside the bank had at least minor wounds.

The main street and First National Bank

Inside the bank, the job was going just as poorly. Charlie Pitts, Bob Younger, and Frank James, their breath reeking of whiskey, swaggered up to the counter and drew their guns on the cashier and two bookkeepers, demanding they open the safe. The gang encountered three men, Joseph Lee Heywood, Alonzo E. Bunker, and Frank J. Wilcox, who all denied being the cashier when told that their bank was being robbed. Jesse told Heywood that he knew he was the cashier and demanded that he open the safe, but Heywood refused. As Frank went to the vault to inspect the safe, Heywood ran toward Frank and shoved him, trying to trap him inside. Frank got away, but not before getting his hand and arm caught in the door. Bob Younger then pushed Heywood to the floor.

The startled employees told them it had a time lock and couldn't be opened. In reality, the safe was closed but unlocked. About $15,000 sat inside, ready for the taking, but the drunken robbers didn't even bother to try the door. Frustrated, the robbers cleared out the cash drawer of $26.70, not noticing that it could be lifted up to reveal another cash drawer that contained $2,000.

One of the bookkeepers tried to grab a pistol from under the counter, but Bob Younger was too quick for him and grabbed the gun first. The three robbers then proceeded to beat up the cashier, demanding that he open the safe. He insisted that there was a time lock and could do nothing. At this point one of the bookkeepers bolted out a side door. Pitts shot him in the shoulder, but the employee still managed to stagger away.

Just then Cole Younger stuck his head in the door. Surrounded by a haze of gun smoke and with blood running down his leg, he shouted, "Come out of the bank! For God's sake, come out, they are shooting us all to pieces!" As the three inside the bank turned to leave, one of them (Cole Younger later hinted it was Frank James) shot Heywood in the head and killed him, a senseless act of murder brought about by whiskey and frustration.

After they came out, it wasn't long before all three were hit by the fusillade coming from the citizens of Northfield. Back outside, a citizen had shot Clell Miller with light birdshot, the ammunition that the shop owner had put in a rifle in all of the confusion. The birdshot ripped at Clell's face and punctured one of his eyes, but he managed to stay on his horse and ride on through town. Anselm Manning, a citizen with a rifle, shot Cole in the shoulder, but Cole stayed on his horse and rode away without looking back. Manning also took out one of the gang's horses, shot Bill Chadwell dead with one shot to the heart, and finished off Clell with a shot that severed an artery in his shoulder. Wheeler, the medical student, had found a rifle and took a position in an upper story window, shot Jim Younger in the shoulder.

As Frank entered the street and climbed on his horse, he was unwittingly walking right into a shooting gallery and was almost immediately shot in the right leg. Jim Younger was shot again in the right shoulder and Bob took cover under a staircase. As Bob tried to shoot from his vantage point, he was shot in the elbow, a wound that would cripple him for the rest of his life. Charlie Pitts was also shot in the leg. Jim took another shot in his leg as Cole circled back to get to Bob. Cole was shot three times, but still managed to grab Bob and the brothers took off after Jesse, Frank, and Jim. As the remnants of the James-Younger Gang bolted out of town, with $26.76 in the bag of loot, the citizens of Northfield threw stones and pitchforks.

As they rode out of town, Bob fainted and had to be held up by his brother Jim. They left behind the bodies of Miller and Stiles, as well as an innocent bystander who had gotten caught in the crossfire. The gang had intended on wrecking the telegraph office on their way out of town, but now there was no time. News of the shootout was soon flashing across the entire state and posses were forming up in all the local towns. Making matters worse, every single member of the gang was injured and they were short a horse. They robbed a farmer of a plough horse, but this animal proved to be slow. Before the sun set, they had had brief encounters with two posses, but neither side took more injuries.

Eventually, three of the gang were dead and the Younger brothers were arrested and given long prison terms. Only Frank and Jesse got away. After the fiasco in Northfield, Frank and Jesse stayed quiet for nearly three years. Northfield was the last straw for Frank, and he was ready to settle in on his farm near Nashville using the alias B.J. Woods. Jesse told everyone he was J.D. Howard, and the two were known by their neighbors only as law-abiding citizens. But as content as Frank was living a quiet life with his family, Jesse was restless. He tried to make money racing horses and playing cards, but he was not successful at either, and his money eventually started to run out. It also began to gnaw at him that he was no longer in the public eye; even his own children had no idea who Jesse James was. At a certain point, Jesse's nature got the best of him, and he became determined to return to life as an outlaw.

In the summer of 1879, Jesse headed back to Missouri to try and form a new gang, but it was nothing like his previous gang, and his recruits had neither the experience nor the loyalty that he had grown accustomed to over the past decade. Nevertheless, James and the new gang went on a crime spree throughout Missouri and the South, robbing a train in what is now Independence, Missouri and the paymaster at a canal project in Killen, Alabama. During another train robbery in Missouri, they killed a passenger and the train's conductor.

By early 1882, Jesse was trying to put together yet another new gang, but he was running out of options. Now just a loose band of common thieves, Jesse was not even sure that he could trust the men in his gang. He grew increasingly paranoid and even murdered one of the members of his gang, Ed Miller. Convinced that Jim Cummins was out to get him, too, Jesse was in the process of hunting him down. The only two men that he thought he could really trust were Bob and Charley Ford. What Jesse did not know when he offered the Fords the chance to take part in robbing the Platte City Bank is that they had already agreed to a deal with Governor Crittenden.

Crittenden

Bob Ford was able to get a meeting with the governor through his sister Martha Bolton, who had been the object of a gun battle with Bob and a man named Dick Liddil, which resulted in the death of Wood Hite. With Bolton's assistance, Bob Ford negotiated a deal with Crittenden, who told him that if James was killed, the reward money that had been put up by the railroads would belong to him. Crittenden also mentioned that if Ford happened to be the one to ensure that Jesse was killed, he had the authority to pardon him. Bob convinced Charley that they should kill Jesse and get the reward money. Incredibly, the governor of Missouri had conspired to murder Jesse James.

On the morning of April 3, 1882, Charley and Bob Ford were at Jesse's home in St. Joseph. Zee prepared breakfast for the men as Jesse got ready for a robbery that he had planned. Charley reportedly broke out into a sweat, causing Zee to comment and ask him if he was sick. Meanwhile, Jesse had taken off his gun belt to avoid drawing too much attention as he went in and out of his house. For Jesse to be without his guns was a rare occasion, but he gave the Fords the opening they had been waiting for. As Jesse climbed on to a chair to dust a picture, Bob and Charley drew their guns and approached him from behind. Bob shot Jesse point blank in the back of the head. Hearing the shot, Zee ran into the room and screamed, "You've killed him." Bob Ford's immediate response was, "I swear to God I didn't." His curious remark aside, Jesse James was dead.

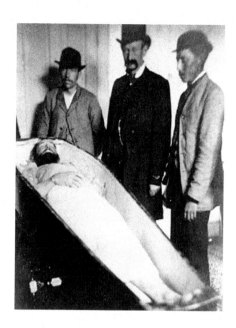

Jesse's body in a coffin

The Ford brothers surrendered to authorities and were convicted of murder, but Crittenden kept his word, and they were promptly pardoned and received some but not all of the $10,000 reward. However, the glory and notoriety they anticipated would come their way didn't materialize in the way they hoped. The Ford brothers initially billed themselves as the men who killed Jesse James and attempted to profit off of it by reenacting the murder and posing for photographs, but as was often the case in Jesse's lifetime, the public sided with him and was horrified at the cowardly way Bob Ford took Jesse's life. Bob was forced to leave Missouri in shame. Four years later, Charley Ford, done in by the stigma attached to what was called one of the most cowardly deeds in Missouri's history, shot himself in the weeds near his home in Richmond, Missouri.

Bob Ford

At the behest of Jesse's mother, the inscription on Jesse's tombstone read, "Jesse W. James. Died April 3, 1882. Aged 34 years, 6 months, 28 days. Murdered by a traitor and a coward whose name is not worthy to appear here."

Like many icons of the Wild West, much of the legend of Jesse James is wrapped up in myth. He lived in an era when Americans on the East Coast clamored for tales of the West, whether the tales were true or not. However, unlike some western icons that were tagged as being outlaws far more dangerous than they really were, Jesse James was built up to be a more chivalrous bandit than he was in real life. The fact is that Jesse James was a cold-blooded killer who did not, contrary to legend, steal from the rich to give to the poor. He robbed the rich and poor alike, all for his own personal gain.

It took very little time for Jesse's family to cash in on his name. His mother was offered $10,000 by a promoter for her son's body, presumably to put the deceased outlaw on public display. Zerelda gave it some consideration, but opted instead to have Jesse buried in her front yard where she could watch over his grave. When sightseers and the curious came by to visit Jesse's final resting place, Zerelda sold them pebbles from the gravesite for a few cents each. When she ran out of pebbles, she replenished her supply from the alley behind her house.

Jesse's widow, Zee James, was offered money to write a book about her husband, but despite needing the money she refused to and would end up dying poor. Jesse's son did, though, writing *Jesse James, My Father* in 1899. The first movie about Jesse appeared in 1908 when *The James Boys of Missouri* was released. The film was 18 minutes long, and taking into account that Jesse was still a sympathetic figure to many, the portrayal of him as an outlaw was done lightly. It was also a successful play for several years.

This began a string of dozens of movie and television portrayals of Jesse or characters based on him that continued into the 21st century. Of all of the movies about him, Jesse's descendants claim that *The Assassination of Jesse James by the Coward Bob Ford*, starring Brad Pitt as Jesse in the last four months of his life, is the most accurate portrayal. The movie was adapted from a novel of the same name. Included in the film is the fact that Bob Ford went to New York to reenact the killing of Jesse James onstage, with his brother Charley playing the role of Jesse.

In the wake of his notorious life and death, Jesse James was portrayed in several different was. Some viewed James as a symbol of resistance against government and industry, turning him into some sort of pre-Progressive Era rebel. Others viewed him as a symbol of the antebellum South whose life of crime was more about avenging the South and their lost way of life.

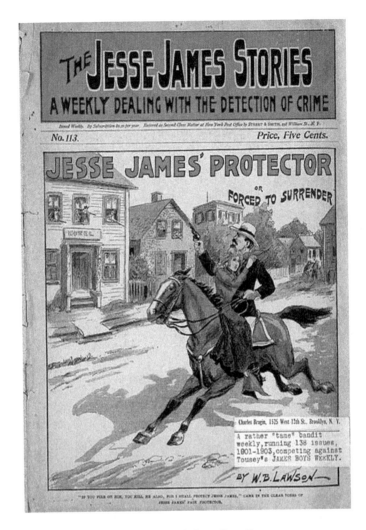

A 1901 dime novel about Jesse James

Jesse's name and likeness have been used to sell dime novels, comic books, and any number of collectibles. Items from lunch boxes to replica badges to shot glasses are highly desirable. Even reproductions of photographs of Jesse in a casket are easily found. In fact, the Jesse James Wax Museum in Stanton, Missouri offers tourists an array of Jesse James souvenirs, while keeping alive the debunked legend that Jesse faked his death and lived until 1948. Northfield, Minnesota has kept their link to Jesse's life alive with the Defeat of Jesse James Days festival, complete with a parade, an arts and crafts festival, and regular reenactments of the bank robbery.

It has taken time for some Americans to relinquish the image of Jesse James as a type of hero, which speaks to the deep wounds of the Civil War and the battle over the future of slavery as much as it does for Jesse's character. That Jesse lived and made his name as an outlaw during a time when there was such fascination with the West helped fuel his own need for attention and, in many respects, validation. Add into the mix the belief by those that sympathized with the Confederacy that he was a hero and the result is a legend.

However, that time has largely passed, and even as James remains perhaps the most famous outlaw of the West, glorified portrayals of him as heroic outlaw are now more about profiting off an interesting story than historical accuracy. New generations of Americans have come to view the antebellum South, the Civil War and the post-war bushwhacking much differently. In that context, Jesse James was hardly a hero, and despite his attempts to portray himself to the contrary, he was not a victim. He was caught up in an era of change and did not like the change he saw.

Online Resources

Other books about the Civil War by Charles River Editors

Other books about the James Brothers on Amazon

Bibliography

Brownlee, Richard S. *Gray Ghosts of the Confederacy: Guerilla Warfare in the West, 1861–1865.* Baton Rouge: Louisiana State University Press, 1984.

Brooksher, William Riley. *Bloody Hill: The Civil War Battle of Wilson's Creek.* Washington, D.C.: Brassey's, 1995.

Castel, Albert E. and Thomas Goodrich. *Bloody Bill Anderson: The Short, Savage Life of a Civil War Guerrilla.* Stackpole Books, 1998.

Kerby, Robert L. *Kirby Smith's Confederacy: The Trans-Mississippi South, 1863-1865.* London: University of Alabama Press, 1972.

Koblas, John. *Faithful unto Death: The James-Younger Raid on the First National Bank, Northfield, Minnesota, September 7, 1876.* Northfield, MN: Northfield Historical Society, 2001.

Lemon, John Jay. *The Northfield Tragedy.* St. Paul, MN: Privately published, 1876. Reprinted in London by Westerners Publications Ltd., 2001.

Leslie, Edward. *The Devil Knows How to Ride: The True Story of William Clarke Quantrill and His Confederate Raiders.* New York: Da Capo Press, 1996.

McCorkle, John. *Three Years with Quantrill.* Norman: University of Oklahoma Press, 1992.

McLachlan, Sean. *American Civil War Guerrilla Tactics.* Oxford, UK: Osprey Publishing, 2009.

McLachlan, Sean. *The Last Ride of the James-Younger Gang: Jesse James and the Northfield Raid 1876.* Oxford, UK: Osprey Publishing, 2012.

Stiles, T.J. *Jesse James: Last Rebel of the Civil War.* London: Jonathan Cape, 2003.

U.S. War Department. *The War of the Rebellion: A Compilation of the Official Records of the Union and Confederate Armies.* Washington, D.C.: Government Printing Office, 1888.

Watts, Hamp B. *The Babe of the Company: An Unfolded Leaf from the Forest of Never to-be-forgotten Years.* Fayette, MO: Democrat-Leader Press, 1913.

Wybrow, Robert J., editor. *From the Pen of a "Noble Robber": The Letters of Jesse Woodson James, 1847-1882.* Privately printed, n.l., 2003.

Yeatman, Ted. *Frank and Jesse James: The Story Behind the Legend.* Nashville: Cumberland House, 2000.

Younger, Cole. *The Story of Cole Younger, by Himself: Being an Autobiography of the Missouri Guerrilla Captain and Outlaw, his Capture and Prison Life, and the Only Authentic Account of the Northfield Raid Ever Published.* Chicago, Illinois: The Henneberry Company 1903.